TRAVEL IN MY BORROWED LIVES

ALSO BY DONALD EVERETT AXINN

poetry

Sliding Down the Wind
The Hawk's Dream and Other Poems
Against Gravity
The Colors of Infinity
Dawn Patrol
The Latest Illusion
Change as a Curved Equation
El sueño del halcón
El sueño del halcón (Ediciones El Tucán de Virginia)
Walking Through the Night
Caminando a través de la noche (Ediciones El Nocedal)

fiction

Spin
The Ego Makers

TRAVEL IN MY BORROWED LIVES

New and Selected Poems

Donald Everett Axinn

Introduction by Jay Parini

Arcade Publishing
New York

Copyright © 2008 by Donald Everett Axinn
Introduction copyright © 2008 by Jay Parini

All rights reserved. No part of this book may be reproduced in any form or by any electronic or mechanical means, including information storage and retrieval systems, without permission in writing from the publisher, except by a reviewer who may quote brief passages in a review.

FIRST EDITION

Library of Congress Cataloging-in-Publication Data

Axinn, Donald E.
  Travel in my borrowed lives : new and selected poems / Donald Everett Axinn. — 1st ed.
    p. cm.
  ISBN 978-1-55970-895-1 (alk. paper)
  I. Title.

PS3551.X5T73 2008
811'.54—dc22   2008031187

Published in the United States by Arcade Publishing, Inc., New York
Distributed by Hachette Book Group USA

Visit our Web site at www.arcadepub.com

10 9 8 7 6 5 4 3 2 1

Designed by API

EB

PRINTED IN THE UNITED STATES OF AMERICA

To Joan, as always and as ever, my close companion and wife. She continues to sparkle. Her inviolable reasoning, challenges, good humor, and love make all the difference.

A good traveler is one who does not know where he is going, and a perfect traveler does not know where he came from.
—Lin Yutang

The universe is a strange place. We are children here at best, ignorant of our origins, our future, or even the right questions to ask.
—Dennis Overbye

What is life? It is a flash of a firefly at night. It is the breath of a buffalo in wintertime. It is the little shadow which runs across the grass and loses itself in the sunset.
—Crowfoot

I do not understand the process of imagination, though I know I am very much at its mercy. I feel that these ideas are floating around in the air and they pick me to settle upon.
—Joseph Heller

The poem is a spirit. It comes we know not whence. It will not speak at our bidding, nor answer in our language. The poem is not our servant; it is our master.
—A. C. Bradley

CONTENTS

Acknowledgments	xv
Publication History	xvii
Author's Note	xix
Introduction by Jay Parini	xxi

SLIDING DOWN THE WIND (1978)

Roman Roads	3
Down on the Beach	4
Over the Atlantic	5
Oh, Stand Quietly in Salt Water	7
Land of My Fathers	8
New Hampshire Summer Sunday	10
Yesterday's Touchdown	13
Saturday's Black Hole	15

THE HAWK'S DREAM (1982)

Travel in My Borrowed Lives	19
The Hawk's Dream	23
Rachel	25
Salmon Run	27
True Love	29
Appointment in Samarra	30
Barrier Beach	33
Land of Dixieland	34
Saturday Night on the Desert, March 1938	36
"Mountain that was God"	37

AGAINST GRAVITY (1986)

Impossible Tasks	41
Tree	43
Genesis	45
Stalls	47
Clouds	49
Forgetting Jesse Carpenter	50
Turn-On	52
Late Monday Afternoon, Just Before the Rain	54
Time to Fly	56

THE COLORS OF INFINITY (1990)

The Hunter	61
A Father Remembered	63
Death of the Son	65
The Bull Comes to Pamplona	67
The Colors of Infinity	69
Kiss	70
Birth of Quasars	71

THE LATEST ILLUSION (1995)

A Miniature Life	75
Electrons and Beaver Ponds	76
Vietnam	78
Byrd, Richard Evelyn, Rear Admiral, U.S.N. —Imagined, from His Diary	80
George "Ace" Alligator (Mississippiensis), Now Residing in Florida	84

This Is What You Get	86
On Being Stoic	87
Amelia Earhart	89
Tracks of the Father, Tracks of the Son	94
This Way to Morning	96
The Reading	97
Pilot	98
This One Aspect	100

CHANGE AS A CURVED EQUATION (2002)

Change as a Curved Equation	103
The Way Forward, the Way Back	106
Until He Asked Me	108
First Love	109
Yaqui Universe	111
Makah Country	112
Mathematics for a Rainy Morning	114

WALKING THROUGH THE NIGHT (2006)

Jones Beach	117
Walking Through the Night	118
Elegy for Bob Johnson	119
Discover the Air	121
Biplane Pilot	123

NEW POEMS (2008)

I Will Lie Down by an Honest Stream	127
The Seasons, Northern Hemisphere	129

First the Clowns	130
There Is More to Tell	131
Immigrant	132
The Weather	133
Why Because	134
Phlox	135
How Carefully I Study Her Sleep	136
The Bed	137
A Certain Truth	138
Summer Morning	140
Signs and Signals	141
College Reunion	142
Friends	144
What I See	145
Security	146
Bare Essentials	147
Siblings	148
Come with Me	149
Flight to Middlebury in a Boeing Biplane	151
Old Man Greets a Small Boy	155
January Daybreak on Long Island Sound	157
Atlantic Sky 33,000 Feet on Delta #73, Istanbul to JFK	158
Across the Grand Canyon at 39,000 Feet	159
Day of the Maccabees, Masada, 164 B.C.E	160
Portovenere ("Sinum Spedia")	161
Countries We Choose to Visit	162
The Tide on St. Simon's	163

Nevada Through a Jet Window	164
Apache	165
Navajo	166
Song of the Sioux	167
Abanaki	168
Cheyenne	169
Comeback	170
Pilot After Flying Through a Storm	171
Fixed Relationships	172
All Thoughts	173

ACKNOWLEDGMENTS

It's important to acknowledge those who, in so many ways, have helped and influenced my writing. They are many and include Jay Parini, Robert Pinsky, Charles Wright, John Elder, Meghan Curley, Miguel Ángel Zapata, Nelson DeMille, Susan Isaacs, Dick and Jeannette Seaver, Leo Guthart, Raymond Cross, Wyche Fowler, Jack Bierwirth, Kim Sparks, and Reeve Lindbergh. And the inimitable Beverly Carr.

Last but by no means least, my children—Meredith, Allison, Michael, Jennifer, Jamie, and Peter—and the rest of my magnificent family and exceptional friends. You know who you are. I am blessed to have you.

PUBLICATION HISTORY

My appreciation to the editors of the following publications, in which these poems previously appeared:

Antaeus	"Byrd, Richard Evelyn"
Confrontation	"Stalls"
Distinction	"Wings"
Long Island Quarterly	"A Miniature Life"
	"Jones Beach"
Middlebury magazine	"The Colors of Infinity"
	"College Reunion"
	"Electrons and Beaver Ponds"
Nature Conservancy magazine	"Down on the Beach"
Newsday	"Saturday's Black Hole"
New York Times	"True Love"
Pearl Street Press	"Travel in My Borrowed Lives"
	"Rachel"
Phi Beta Kappa *Key Notes*	"Tree"
Spruce Creek Update	"Discover the Air"
	"George 'Ace' Alligator"
	"Biplane Pilot"
	"Walking Through the Night"
	"Salmon Run"
	"Come with Me"
	"Atlantic Sky"
	"Roman Roads"

	"Impossible Tasks"
	"The Bed"
	"First the Clowns"
	"I Will Lie Down"
	"Until He Asked Me"
Sunstorm	"The Hawk's Dream"
Transatlantic Steamer /	"El sueño del halcón"
Vapor transatlántico	
Underwood Review	"First Love"
Writer's Forum	"This Is What You Get"
	"Saturday Night on the Desert"
	"Change as a Curved Equation"

AUTHOR'S NOTE

The poems presented in this volume are the winners in an arduous contest as to which ones would make the cut. I apologize to the "losers," trying to placate them with the fact that the author's judgment can often be suspect. Those presented here refused to be abandoned. Some have been slightly revised—a word, a phrase, some punctuation.

I don't remember exactly when it happened. The Muse, in the form of a very devoted and provocative friend, suggested (actually, insisted) that I could create the bridge between conscious and subconscious, normally in dreams, if I would sit quietly and touch thoughts, feelings, and fantasies through the pen in my hand. (Most of the poems were written on an old Sears typewriter.) "You will learn a lot about yourself," she promised.

What came out is what can be called the expurgation, the initial commitment to expression. It then became necessary to craft the initial drafts into respectable pieces of literature.

And so it began, much to my surprise, because I had never thought of myself as a writer. My friend, sadly, has been gone for many decades, but her spirit continues to reside in the Muse. And subject to her moods and when she desires, she sits on my shoulder or on my head and whispers all kinds of things in my ear. (Some are much too personal to share here.) I learned long ago that I have no choice but to do her bidding.

She also demands an excruciatingly careful examination of every idea, every line, every word. Rewriting a poem twenty or thirty times has been surprisingly fulfilling. I enjoy immensely getting her to finally nod her head in approval. And then I can nod mine, too.

D. E. A.

INTRODUCTION

Poetry is a language adequate to experience, and the range of a poet's career will vary with the range of experience that he or she faces, directly or indirectly. Donald Everett Axinn has been writing poems for nearly half a century, and he has faced up to many things. This volume of new and selected poems is a testament to his steady and evolving vision, his ability to record what he has seen. *Travel in My Borrowed Lives* brings together a wide selection of his best work, drawn from different places in his writing life. But the stamp of individuality—the personal voice of the poet—lives on every page. Axinn shows an admirable consistency in his very human concerns: his love of nature, his affection for family and friends, his wish to explore regions of mind as well as regions of sky.

Axinn is a businessman and pilot as well as a poet and novelist, and has pushed himself to the limit in these different fields. In the title poem of an early book, "The Hawk's Dream," he sounds a deeply personal note:

> I am
> spawned by
> sun and wind;
> each night
> when day sleeps,
> I dream
> of a white hawk
> who
> dreams of me.

He is, of course, himself the white hawk, taking a wide view of the world. This is a book of explorations and aerial surveys, and readers will find a wide variety of settings and occasions. There are love poems here, as in the beautiful "First Love," and poems that express the ineffable love we feel for children, as in "Rachel," one of the most delicate of lyrics in this collection. "Death of the Son" is a fierce and compelling poem about making peace with one's father—a subject which Axinn returns to inexorably as he tries to come to terms with the strong father who played such a vivid role in his life. Indeed, Axinn examines the many angles of this life, its origins (in Eastern Europe) and trajectory, in many of these poems, such as "Signs and Signals," where he writes, "I descend from a line that courses from one generation / To the next." These angles create shapes and forms on the page, as a life begins to fall into places in the lines of poetry.

Quite often, Axinn contemplates the universe in large terms, always with a note of wry self-scrutiny, a sense of pervasive doubt: "I do not know if anything exists / past the last galaxy," he writes in "Impossible Tasks." In each of these poems, he hopes to "describe elementary parts of the world," as he writes in "Siblings." This is a bold venture, and one that holds our attention.

As a pilot-poet (a version of the "white hawk"), Axinn surveys the scene below and around him. He delights in nature, as poets have always done from the time of Chaucer. I always admire Axinn's fresh, concrete sense of the world, as in "The Seasons, Northern Hemisphere," where he writes about the ground in winter, "topped with cool gentle snow," or the ground in "spring's sassy days," or in summer, "When time fills up its flushed cup to brimming." In a lovely poem called "Summer Morning" he notes how the fog "imitates the mist and the mist the fog." It's a playful poem, in which the sun becomes "that sly old man."

The settings of these poems shift from Long Island (as in the lovely "January Daybreak on Long Island Sound") to Vermont, widening to include many parts of the world. Axinn has been a traveler from the start, and these poems traverse a range of cultures as well as places, with some fascinating poems (as in "Song of the Sioux," "Apache," or "Navajo") revealing a deep interest in Native American themes and traditions. Here is a man who has looked at the world from many angles, always with the bright curiosity of a child, with a sense of gathering wisdom, which is the result of experience in the world at large.

The wisdom in these poems is often moving, as in "Fixed Relationships," where Axinn contemplates with a certain whimsical flourish the hard realities of time and place: "At my age I shouldn't protest so much," he writes, "but certain mysteries remain like old companions." At the end of this fine poem he says, "Enigmas used to peek around corners." But these enigmas have become more urgent now, and one feels the urgency in his newest poems, as in "Bare Essentials," where he faces up to what is real, or what cannot be unseen, unstated. He addresses the reader boldly here: "Hold my hand, you'll face some truths: / Ecstasy, escape, errors, time, limitations." These are some of the many aspects of experience that readers will encounter in these poems. A large and terrifying journey is traced by Donald Everett Axinn in this work, but it remains an essential journey, as the evidence of these poems demonstrates.

—Jay Parini

SLIDING DOWN THE WIND

ROMAN ROADS

In Rome, Rome, Rome, in Rome
                  all roads lead to
Rome, Roma; roads to roam
                  roaming roads in
Roman Roma, roving
                  roads, Romany
Roma, these Roman roads
                  rambling roads
Ramble in Rome, Respighi's
                  Rome, remember?
Remembering Rome
                  radiant Rome
Rococo Roma,
                  roaring Roman
Regiments, rivaling,
                  remove Roman
Right, roaring righteous
                  ravish the ripe;
Roman roads, oh help me,
                  all my roaming
Roads lead to
                  me.

DOWN ON THE BEACH

I see time:
    ice cakes and snow puddings,
    the winter's ingredients
that remind me
who the hell I am,
    and who I am
    not.
Some fall wind stacked
the leaves against the weeds
    readying the ground
    for winter brown;
The year dies—and
if spring wasn't somewhere in my head
    the final ugliness would be
    the final ugliness;
But, I watch
the magic show,
    clap like a child,
    excited, laughing.
The Magic Show.

OVER THE ATLANTIC

ocean spread so far that
land is only an idea,
a memory of some myth we need
    to repeat over and over

endless bed of salted sapphire waves
partially camouflaged by bulbous
cumulus clouds, pretty cauliflower
buds ready to be eaten, a huge
blanket looking like a brightly
    patched blue and white quilt

then
    wild drunken thoughts, tumbling
through flower vegetable patch far below
or as in my dreams flying strong and free
gliding, soaring on winglike arms;
suddenly Icarus, falling, shrieking
forgetting
    all direction to the stars
where we are born
over and over again
forgetting
    how loving so much feels that
    nothing else really matters
until
    I grab at white stratus whiskers

whispering an ancient Hebrew melody and
chant with all the prophets learning
secrets; no longer so lonely
    I stop shaking and shrug off that
bottomless whirlpool of black pitch,
that silent terror gone.

soon I know
    I have been away five thousand years,
traveling through all the parched deserts
of Sinai, learning the Covenant
and Torah commandments, wandering
the wilderness of the Diaspora, struggling with
Joshua into Canaan, becoming a Maccabee,
fighting Macedonians in Jerusalem and Romans
at Masada, and begetting Abraham and Isaac and
Jacob, then Joseph and Moses and David and
Solomon, their sons
    and my sons

now
    in this dazzling and holy place
where I sense my God who decides
what is a Wednesday or sunlight,
whether forty-seven is the middle
    or the end.

OH, STAND QUIETLY IN SALT WATER

All hail to these two
Gray boulders, proud but scarred,
Hoary and pockmarked by
Barnacles, those ancient
Hangers-on fouled by
Guiltless gulls laughing loudly.

    Oh, stand quietly
    In salt water, holding on
    Like friends who have become
    Very old together,
    Sharing cold misery
    Remembering warmth and smiles,

Grasping wildly
For the galloping clock but soon
Silenced by the spinning
Seasons, until all their
Vanity is vomited,
Tears are tasteless,

    And the tide has gone
    Somewhere else forever.

LAND OF MY FATHERS

sliding deep into moistened
pregnant soil, fingers spread
reaching instinct imbedded
by ancestors breathing blood into
the brown, plenteous potato
source and substance for survival

guns like angry sabers tearing,
teeth dripping red flesh
piling young bodies into bales
of wheat, the grain crumbling

scream, Russian peasant, cries of
Beshenkovitchi, burning in snowy
wastes flaming with clenched fists
whipped by laughing Cossacks who
rape daughters and wives their
faces contorted, remembering
promises once secret now destroyed

but spring returns forgetting
the blood of its sons soaked into
the steppes, and demands strong hands
to plant the new crop of babies

a soft song is heard over this land
that cannot be sung but we do try
exactly as our fathers did
on their knees, weeping next
to our mothers no longer able
to make milk, hold us or bake bread

NEW HAMPSHIRE SUMMER SUNDAY

"Ayup. Plymouth is up on the road
Above Meredith and Laconia."
Quiet hangs there gently through stately pines and
 maples,
The calm rye grass cradling the soft warmth of summer.

"And off Route 25 where Smith Bridge Road rambles
Not over but through Smith Bridge, covered not for
Tourists but sometime back last century
When they worked the fields and watched the weather.

"Then bear left past the young corn tended by old hands
Over to John Fraser's airfield, all green sodded
Like they were back before macadam strips or
Concrete dashed with tire marks marking landings pilots
Would rather forget; they don't seem to feel the wind
 anymore."

Pipers and Cessnas surround Fraser's field but their
Captains bark no instructions, no motors mar
The gentle Sunday afternoon, at least not today.
"Nope, there aren't any planes for rent," says John Fraser.

On, on toward Plymouth town past fathers patiently
Showing sons how to mow, much like when Indian
Fathers would teach theirs to corn, dance, hunt and wait.

Down on Baker River sands, mothers remind young
     daughters
That a swim suit top does what it is supposed to.

The four-seasoned buildings of Plymouth State College
Now sun themselves and rest, emptied of scholars off to
     work or
Play or both, and two fine Mobil stations stand
Opposite each other like squared-off chess knights.

"That 1861 house there sure needs some paint.
(New Hampshire houses always look better spanking
     white.)
The Plymouth Inn is all whitened up but
Somebody'll have to paint in the guests."

Up High Street to Red Gate Farm Antiques;
An old radio was turned on with
The Shadow and Lamont Cranston knowing what
"Good and evil lurks in the minds of men."

Well, the Plymouth Theater gets them for either
The 6:45 or the 9:00 show—it isn't much but
Things could be a lot worse off.
"See over there that Miller factory building standing
Four stories high—The Home of Miller Shoe Trees,
Even with a picture on the sign in case
Nobody is sure what they looked like."

The Christian Science Reading Room is closed now,
But looks laconically at that ideal couple,
The Pemigewasset National Bank and
The Plymouth Guaranty Savings Bank
Comfortable with each other after all these years.

YESTERDAY'S TOUCHDOWN

The steady smacking of boat bottom
Like a kettle drum
Rolling to the muted
Choral rounds of my motor,
Faithful but mindless,
Servant to my demands.

    Alone and undivided,
    The world nowhere in sight
    My ears listening without complaint
    As my eyes select a 90-degree course.

"Oh, run on, run on,
Good friend, for I'm blessed by
Neptune and shall not be
Ulysses needing an odyssey
To test my fortunes."

    But fantasy inebriates my view
    PT boat twists jaggedly
    Like a game-winning quarterback
    Toward Japanese carrier
    Impervious to shells and Ack-Ack—
    Fire Starboard One!
    Fire Two!

It blows apart and like
Yesterday's touchdown we outrun
Destroyers, zig the Zeroes,
Zag the Kamikazes
Getting away and winning.

But now it's all gone and I'm afraid
Hanging rolls of flabby gray haze
Wreck chances to see where to go
And compass becomes a god to whom
Offerings may have to be made.

SATURDAY'S BLACK HOLE

Friday was spent
    wondering if Joan is pregnant (she is),
    renting that old vacant building,
    arguing about the rent and tenant changes,
    hoping the bank makes the loan,
    driving too fast into Manhattan,
    deciding to get Mike a stuffed toy, too.

Today Walter Sullivan
    writes in the *New York Times* about
    a "black hole" in the heavens
    that swallows light and matter,
    a 6,000,000,000,000-mile-long
    vacuum cleaner (nonelectric),
    slightly larger than those noisy
    street tanks sucking in November leaves
    or my kitchen sink complaining as it
    drains, noisily sucking in last night's
    dishwater left there by some woozy host.

Casually, back on page 62
    he says (between yawns) that the
    black hole is where all the missing
    matter is going, but only a fraction of
    what can be seen or they know exists
    period, end of article. Thanks a lot.

Come on, Mr. Sullivan,
>I know where the leaves and water went.
>I'm not some schoolchild who has to
>accept your black answers to my white
>questions, as if you know everything.

You could, Mr. Sullivan,
>really tell me about the black hole
>write again next Saturday
>this time on page one,
>especially about all the light and sound
>that matters at the bottom of the
>black hole, where the bottom goes and
>how in the world she got pregnant.

THE HAWK'S DREAM

TRAVEL IN MY BORROWED LIVES

The mist blushes,
Then curtsies to a sun
That climbs over and commands
These hills frosted with bird calls.
There is a smell this morning of
Chekhov's *The Cherry Orchard*.
      See,
There Ranevskaya and Trofimoff,
Rocking back and forth
On the plains of their lives,
Palms open,
Unwilling to listen as the old order changes
And unable to stop the sale of their heritage.

      Or, across the planet,
The set of *Gone with the Wind*.
Cocky young men gallop up to
Tara, pushing aside nests
Of magnolia mossed on their faces,
Hot to drink mint juleps three centuries old.
      Or, if you prefer,
Peach blossoms dripping on Rhett Butler,
Laughing on his magnificent
Black stallion; yes, dark, grinning
Rhett Butler pouring sweet songs
Through his mustache and owled smile.

       He gives a damn.
He imagines Scarlett chattering
With her suitors. But she is not
Penelope, nor is he Odysseus.

       How perceptive
And almost imperious you are to have
So much of these places in you! And
Your clothes, so crisp and fresh
Like the earth under your feet.

       You have
Hung up your rector's collar and dance
Pink waltzes, sweat satin gavottes,
Or jump into blackened boots, down
On your haunches, doing the kazotsky.
Go anywhere with your passport of
Green optimism, Raleigh carrying
Scented letters from Elizabeth
       On your heart of whispers.
Your rapier need never be used.
You have your royal commission!

You love this path of swollen leaves
Fused with all your remembrances.
It leads up and down through old Stuart
And Tudor lacework villages. Cobblestones
Echo horseshoes prancing around
The square. Well water glistens sweet and pure.

Apple pies cool on window ledges
For lovers who will traffic with
Bodiced and bonneted maidens gossiping inside.
        Keep on going,
Dreamer, around to the bells of this
Church tower, gothic and pointed,
Like your purpose. Engrave a prayer
Skipped out of France on your way back
From the Crusades.

        Yes! I do know you!
We have spilled portions on stories we have
Digested, tales caked in the mud of travels,
Epics washed in the salt of Malta.
Our ship skated across Styx and Cocytus
On winds poured into jeweled goblets,
Winds of red wine that tasted
Like blood, but we did not know the difference.

        Take off your dented
Armor, sit a while. There's a cardinal
With a message: his wife hides from us!
She was warned against the Cossacks,
Against the graycoats and bluecoats
Of Gettysburg. She is Russian and runs
From the Cossacks. She gathers her children
And gambles on America. They will lose
Their hoarseness, learn how numbers will
Carry them to the moon. They will find
All the bright places in their myths

And walk the rails laid down by the Italians
And Chinese and Irish somewhere between
Springfield and Denver.

      Yes, your grandmother
Was Russian and a believer. Now we can
Improvise angles that complement
And buy rectangles we will build into a house.
We will plan errors because we have not
Traveled. What? All right,
      One last story:
Your helmet and goggles intrigue me,
Even though your jodhpurs are torn.
Yes, I know what happened after
You crashed in the jungle, searching for
Beauty. Christopher Caldwell died in Spain.
You survived your unconscious, but then
      You always do.

This morning is bright and enters
Without nightmares.
Go! Be what you want. You have
What you need. Run or walk
But don't beg. Never beg for a ride.
      Travel on your own.

THE HAWK'S DREAM

The sun prints
contours and edges,
defining trees,
houses, cars, people;
the shadows create
memories from a life
I may have
borrowed, an accident
that now includes me.

The wind stacks
leaves in corners,
later puffs snow around
plants, like feathers
quilted for winter
sleep; shadows
disappear then appear,
soundless gusts
from an insistent sun.

>   I am
>   spawned by
>   sun and wind;
>   each night
>   when day sleeps,
>   I dream

of a white hawk
who
dreams of me.

RACHEL

And finally
you arrived,
breathless,
after waiting
for months
in the wet warmth,
becoming you
inside your mother.

And then
you cried,
that first breath
pushed through
vocal chords
you learned
could be used
from then on.

We heard you,
Rachel,
mother first,
through tears
that were the first thing
she offered you,
tears she had been saving up
and didn't know
were there,

tears
that made her milk flow,
milk
that will bond you
together as in
no other way.

And then
when she held you,
you stopped crying
because you knew
she would be yours
from then on.

And I cried too,
because already
I loved you
even though
we had just met.

I didn't
know who
you would be,
Rachel;
I waited a long time
for you,
and it was dark
where I was, too.

SALMON RUN

years
after   swimming out of   the sweet
into   the salt
years
after   wandering   the North Pacific
circling   fighting   surviving

    I
    flash   through rivers
    threaded   with claws
    men   then bears
    try   to   tear me
    my   pink flesh
    bleeds
    dripping   hurting

I
am   flopping   back   home
safely
to   streams
calmer
at   their beginnings

    I
    sense   you   waiting there
    in   the shallows

```
your eggs        all
plumped up         you
swish      your rainbowed tail
we      slip      into the pit
we      mate       I       die
```

TRUE LOVE

Night has shut off the light.
The crickets are my eyes.
    They tell me the tales
    They would have me know,
Of shining knights
        On horse by the road,
        Silk scarves tied
        Tight to lances.
Of fiery dragons,
        Nicely groomed,
        All green and smiling,
        Breath smoky sweet,
    Who loved the knights
    Who killed the dragons.

If you listen carefully
The crickets always stop talking
    At the sound
    Of approaching horses.
Some say
        The crickets see
        The knights.
That may be.
    But they don't see
    The dragons anymore.

APPOINTMENT IN SAMARRA

". . . and one of them, on seeing
Death, runs away to Samarra.
'That's strange,' Death says
to the other, 'that's where
I have an appointment to meet with her.'"

I

She hears the wind
Pour through the oaks,
How it organizes the branches,
Stirring the leaves that make
A confusion of small sounds
Against each other.

I must tell her
The treetops sway in sections
Like undulating ballet dancers
Moving in waves.
She nods and muses quietly,
"Yes, of course."

I must tell her
Of the ravens
That took her eyes,
That fly soundlessly,

One by one
To the bird feeder,
Taking turns with blue jays and cardinals,
Offering colors
She has not seen
Since she was three.

II

And a storm follows.
She runs wildly,
Trying to escape
Each clap of thunder,
Unsure where the lightning
Will strike.
She bangs into brush and
Trips over stones.
I call out to guide her
But she cannot tell
Where things are
In the darkness.

III

Sometimes she feels
My mouth and face
With her fingers.
She can tell me what I see
When I have not even noticed.

She knows more quickly
When the sun flames softly,
But not where it casts
Deep tones on an aging afternoon.

At night I whisper that
She loves more fully than I do,
That less is often more.
She smiles and tells me, yes,
She hears and smells and tastes better,
But that she would trade it all
For twenty minutes
In front of my mirror.

BARRIER BEACH

The beach is a vigilant guardian,
Great arms spread out, protecting all behind.
November sits on the sand, taking its turn.
The people have returned to the mainland.

The ocean is chafed by the wind and
Bares an angry face of white waves.
A handful of gulls are bounced around
So much they finally jump up and leave.

A small trawler plows a section off
The sand bar, dragging for blues and weaks.
Sometimes it drops into farmer furrows, the rigging
Appears like broken crosses on a battlefield.

White-necked scoters fly low and fast, oblivious
To the wind that is ceaseless, that pushes
The water out of the sea up onto the beach.
It does until the November moon, no longer

Amused by the wind, pulls the water back
Down into the sea, back off the beach that's
Left only with marks and remnants
Like a lover who has come and gone.

LAND OF DIXIELAND

Hey, listen: you can hear them, can't you?
There, around the corner,
those seven sounds scrambling
in the dank mustiness
of Preservation Hall.

Here, get a little closer.
That horn is Percy Humphrey's
love, and
notes stand up,
at different heights,
like choir boys
marching with shiny icons.

The melody oozes,
fingers tap on tabletops,
bodies sway, controlled by the rhythm.

Well, they've finished
"Beale Street Blues."
It hangs in the smoke,
then blends into laughter and
noises from chairs scratching
against the tilted floor.
Waiters hover like birds,
asking for drink orders before the next set.

They start again,

slowly at first,
the music shimmering like that "sexy" dancer
across the street,
who rolls her shoulders and then her hips.

Sweet Emma takes another last sip,
slides to the mike;
"… *don't the moon look lonesome*
shining through the trees?
Don't a man seem lonesome
when his woman packs to leave?"

New Orleans bards and balladeers,
hear the cries of the Quarter.
And years earlier,
of cotton and whips,
run and hide.
Now it's all newly painted
even though some buildings
only have fronts:
nothing is permitted to spoil
the Mardi Gras.

But *he's* there,
around the corner,
legless,
begging on his skateboard.

He's still there.
Waiting.

SATURDAY NIGHT ON THE DESERT, MARCH 1938

The moon is fully turned on over
Fort Huachuca. On a distant ridge
A coyote yaps and whines his serenade
To an audience of barrel cacti.
The scooped-out valley south to Naco
Looks like the Copernicus Crater,
Scarred with faults and bouldered rubble.
Tonight Bisbee must be an erupting
Volcano of beer. The copper miners are
Rolling in the lava, its froth washing
The dank and grime from their eyes.

In this last hour before taps,
The all-black cavalry battalion
Repolishes its boots for the Colonel's
Weekly Review on the parade grounds.
Ernesto lies against a very old fig tree,
Dreaming a cowboy's dream of Nogales' whores
With perfumed smiles and swooshing skirts.
Soon he mounts his horse, heading west
Up into Carr Canyon where that lost
Calf might be. And the coyote leaves
The ridge, following a faint scent.

"MOUNTAIN THAT WAS GOD"

"I am Gray Fox. I live and fish
the Nisqually and the Yakima.

"My grandfather told me of Rainier,
'Mountain that was God,' land pushed
so high men would see her forever.

"My grandfather told me when the rains stop and
it is clear, I will see her haloed head poking
through quilted blankets of clouds.

"I will see her shoulders are the bulging
muscles of her blue-iced glaciers.
I will see her spines rise like the dinosaur's into

"Rocky spires that punch through fields
of fractured snow. Her cheeks are craggy
With cracked calluses. I have stood on her
bouldered chins, trying to understand.
Grandfather told me the tales of how she has been
burned by centuries of the Sun's gas-fired breath.

"It is good when she is calm and pleased
with us; then there are many salmon."

AGAINST GRAVITY

IMPOSSIBLE TASKS

For Meri, Allie, Mike, Jenny

I cannot teach you
    about death.
I cannot pass on to you
    what I do not know.
I can only imagine what
    the beyond is,
  where we have never been,
  where we hope something occurs,
    like light or time.

I do not know if anything exists
    past the last galaxy,
  in that void hardly contemplated.
How many is the infinite number
  of oxygen and hydrogen atoms
  that join to sponsor water
    in perfect symbiosis?
    And in greened Iowa,
The kernels of yellow-gold corn, as many
  as the uncounted stars in the uncounted
    galaxies?

Oh, but I will tell you
    that if death were
  an enemy, I would fight like hell.

We would engage in epic combat,
                roiling on
    boiling seas, clanging underneath
    Wagnerian evergreens, hurling thunderbolts
            across mountains.

  My blows would be Herculean,
            my rage unstoppable,
My victory complete, death killed and
    cast under your feet.

But it may even be that death is simply
             the nothingness beyond,
    beyond numbers, beyond thought,
          beyond fantasy,
Where time transcends anything
        we can comprehend.

  Or death may live in a place
Together with life, where colors are soft
           and warmed with hope,
    smells the sweetness of pleasure,
Touch the security of faith, of peace,
          taste the sharp cockiness
    of confidence, and
Sight the laughter and tears, the love
        I have had
    since you came from that other place,
To be carried with me here and where
          I will go.

TREE

For Nadine Heyman

Do you remember when
I was little? You were my
comforter a canopy with
wings spread wide, who listened when
I couldn't talk to *them*.
You were my refuge from spring rains,
summer's scorch, and in winter
flakes of wet snow. I would stand
tight to your rough skin, your
thick body blocked me from the iced winds.

They couldn't hear
our whisperings and the things we shared.

If I cried you would touch me
or do something to make me forget.

When I climbed way up in your arms,
I was taller more powerful
than anyone below.

I always loved you in ways I could
never explain and one day
you said my initials were yours.

I grew up went across
the horizon, planted new trees.

Yesterday I watched them cut
you down, dump you on that
flatbed hearse, your limbs gaping,
graceless uncoordinated, awkward,
sliced into grotesque pieces.

I followed as they carted you
crouched in your embarrassment—
uncovered—onto Main Street
like a freak show for all to see.

But somehow, even after all that
you were still alive juices oozed
out your sheared limbs and you lifted
a few leaves, waved to me into
a last wind. I turned from your
final humiliation
unwilling to witness the very
end after your last gasp when
someone would warm themselves over
your burning bones, perhaps
laugh by the heat from your heart.

GENESIS

For Adam Rosenberg and Lesa Shapiro

You were not
supposed to be here
at the time of my rebirth.
I did not expect
your eyes
Hebrew-blue
that I see
before anything else.
You must have come
straight from
the Psalms and Proverbs
after bathing in
the Pools of Solomon.

They will try
to stop us,
but we will race
beyond their grasp
across the forest floor
past timid ferns
that sway to lute songs
past wildflowers waiting
thousands of years for us.
We shall throw
our pasts away

slip down inside
each other's eyes.
I shall learn about my face
from your fingers.

You will teach me
where warmth is
deep within,
where your shyness waits,
where gravity pulls me.
You make me shiver.
When my words tremble
you unravel them
muted by your faith,
wiping away hesitation
quieting my fears.

I do not know why
you first said,
"Dance with me."
Your eyes
are twin moons
that smile.
They have seen inside
And hint of the future.
We will go then
out there
and dance among the winds.

STALLS

A stall
is a ritual
of flying.

Pilots need to test
the exact moment
when gravity leans on
the plane's nose,
pushes it down
into a fall
and us with it.

To find
that instant when
change is in command,
the wheel or stick
pulled back,
as if we were choosing
to haul ourselves
backward into our pasts.

We point up and up and up
until the instant
we cannot angle any higher.
Forward speed staggers,
time slushes
and we meet that very

second and, like an orgasm exploding,
we tumble from
that held position
wondrously out of control
into the present tense
and then oh and then
into the future.

CLOUDS

are puffed up
tales
telling stories,
illusions
whose time has come,

breaths blown eloquently
by the Creator,
impregnating
the air

the way galaxies
are brushed
across
the cosmos.

FORGETTING JESSE CARPENTER

We did forget your face,
    Jesse.
The one we gave you the
    Bronze Medal for.
When you did those things
    for us in
World War II.

Do you remember him,
    Jesse Carpenter?
No, of course you don't.
    Why should you?
He dropped out in '62, from
    his family.
From the way most of us live.

An alcoholic,
    Jesse.
The street was his home,
    with another vet,
Johnny Lamb, his old buddy in a
    wheelchair he wouldn't
Leave that last very cold night.

He froze about a block from the
    White House.
Where presidents decide how many
    hundreds of billions
Go for dams and defense.
    He was easy to ignore
Out there in the dark.

TURN-ON

This morning darkness lingers . . .
Simple things are hard to describe:
the way the light edges over
night's borders, dawn one step behind,
the sharp, green-black silhouette of
evergreens pressed onto brightening sky,
like the cutouts
I used to make in third grade.

And there's clear, luminescent Venus
hanging from a string
below the sliver moon,
the only lights
still left on the blackness.
It's an odd configuration,
meaning something I don't understand
but meaning something.

Yellows and oranges wake up,
push into the darkness
like consciousness aroused;
magenta flaunts its outrageous pink-blue,
even a band of green, if you look carefully . . .

Across the bay,
fire
climbs the windows of the houses,
dawn shakes loose, clears its sleepy throat.

And yet . . .
There are dim blurs on the water
not wakened by the wind
ruffling the surface,
perhaps flocks of scaup asleep or diving.
I can't be sure.

Before I can tell you
all that I have seen,
this spent night has journeyed on,
chased by morning
and my love that seeks
people, animals, everything—

and especially you.

LATE MONDAY AFTERNOON, JUST BEFORE THE RAIN

We buried you
late Monday afternoon,
Dad,
just before the rain,
but you
weren't really there.
We did it well,
like you lived your life,
now closed inside
the grained oak
coffin.

I looked for you
when I woke this morning
but you were shrouded
in the mist
of your mountains.
I could not hear
what you were
telling me,
the words were all
slurred together.

Now, on this Monday,
a week later,
you would say
I should not be afraid,

that I should
live with the pines
and the hardwoods
as they do
with each other.
I should watch
how the tide changes
and learn the ways
time passes.

I still see you
strong and confident,
high on your horse
the one that did not
permit anyone else.
I remember
what made you
laugh
when you became
angry.
I smell so many
of your smells,
hear your sure voice
in the dark,
miss your man's touch,
bristled kisses
and hugs we renewed
when I too became
a father,
when I too fell
fatally into time.

TIME TO FLY

Soon they come, the pilots,
needing to get off the ground,
gravity oppressive, no longer
acceptable. They gather early
on this flat field, edged with
trees they know mark the limits
of the time they will have
to stop within or rise above.

Light has overpowered darkness,
lifting it off and away for the day.
Two, maybe three or four, congregate,
a circle of comrades,
to poke the earth with small talk,
to share glances of the sky,
to feel the wind replace thoughts
until one says slowly,
as if he had drawn the winning card,
"Looks pretty good, I guess."

Then maybe a scratch behind an ear,
a grin, a nod, a turn toward
the hangar where a biplane
waits and listens.
The pilot rolls open the large doors,
walks to his flying ship,
its smells filling his soul

like an elixir. He stands for a moment
between the wings and fuselage,
rests a hand on the painted fabric,
its feel no longer needing
to be remembered.

THE COLORS OF INFINITY

THE HUNTER

In my cave hungry babies
And a mate believe in me, the hunter.

Soon I descend, watch for lurking
Eyes that will pounce on me if I am reckless.

Wary, I stalk obsessed,
Sharpened wails from the cave behind me.

Eons ago I would have covered myself
With furs, my oily hair matted,

My feet dragging in the mud and dust
Of a land where terror was simpler.

Now I wash and shave, groomed
In pinstripes, a tie covering my jugular.

The spears I use are words carefully thrust,
Couched in smiles designed to disarm.

My quarry is captured and soon bound;
I return with a contract, or an animal

Draped across my powerful shoulders.
And somewhere in other caves,

The cost is hunger, the blood of my stark
Victory unmistakable in frightened eyes.

A FATHER REMEMBERED

A Russian boy long Hasidic curls
Kosher food steerage to America.
You cut and ran through Brooklyn.
Ashcan tops protected your guts.
     Your heart grizzled
     the skin on your fists.
Fights stopped trolley cars: The Irish, Jews, Italians, Poles.
     What bum yelled that!
Then you met her my mother.
Now she searches for you in bed
even the cold one you try to sleep in.
     She lights
candles in your mind
especially on Friday nights.
     She prays to God
     but talks to you
with the shrill voice of the condemned.
I try to make her understand
you no longer hear anything.
     What she really has left of you is
     nothing.
On certain days in summer
     I bury you
     in Beshenkovitchi's
weed-strewn cemetery
that reeks with emptiness.
     Your parents wail

and choke   on their headstones
because you no longer
study the Talmud.
                    Why have you forgotten
everything ends up   vacant and white?
Now   autumn drains my memories of you
as the Russian boy
                    I never was.

DEATH OF THE SON

              It's me,
deserted like your folded shadow

dropped into your tight-lipped voice
blackened under snowy prayer-filled

ground that shrouds the sky. Everything
degenerates: the leather of your cowboy saddle,

your Mexican silver-buckled belt
Mom gave me without expression when you left.

I remember time twitched a little
as we walked the cobblestones

You and your immigrant brothers laid down
in thousands to seal the mud

of your beginning so lumber could be stacked
neatly in piles. The wet smells

of rough Eastern pine and spruce, Western fir
and hemlock, Southern oak, maple, and hickory.

If only I could relearn my small steps
up among those faithful, vigilant boards,

hear you command me out from hiding
places to stand on the edge of nothing,

lurch out unprotected into certain gravity,
then be caught below in the iron of your arms.

The lumberyard lies dead, morning light
has crept in to silence the drowsy owl,

you and I have lost all chance to unspool memory.
At least look at me once more

with your pulled-down face so I can feel
the weight of your collapsed life.

They will bury me just the other side
of this path, where the earth waits

to press me down one final, speechless time.
Then I will watch bats wing continually toward the moon.

THE BULL COMES TO PAMPLONA

For Mike Axinn

There must be some mistake.

    The bull stands confused,
    foreigner in this strange arena,
    banderillas suddenly jabbed,
    hurting like thick syringes.
    Picadors ram dulled lances
    between his shoulders,
    grinding out his power.
    He struggles valiantly
    to lift his head,
    to defend against
    these cultists who demand
    his attention for their rite
    and sanguine sacrifice.

Priests on mounts never offer conversion.

    The bull suppresses rage,
    tries to reason as usual
    but they have judged him
    an infidel.
    He no longer has a choice
    and must accept
    the sword as truth.

>   He thinks of young Isaac
>   but God does not send the lamb.

There is no mistake.

THE COLORS OF INFINITY

beyond cold and comprehension
past stashed universes
where God contemplates
the shapes of cosmic islands
where the dead have escaped
old bones and cacophony

where I almost remember
the tingle of first kisses
my children's uncorrupted faces
slipstreams and winging
into the white mystery of clouds
the musty smells of August's forest floors
smoke and wildflowers

there in that wondrous place
where night and day
are always the same
where the end or the beginning
never matter
there I would bathe in the strong
rich colors of infinity

KISS

I have examined your mouth,
searching where your words are born,
grown wet and warm
in the dark placenta of your mind.

I am drawn unswervingly toward them,
my answer to kiss you,
the muted wind watching
the small lantern of our universe.

BIRTH OF QUASARS

Astronomers create computer models
of young blue-hot galaxies
        colliding,
           pitching billions of stars
           out of comfortable orbits.
They remind us that swirling gases—
        the stuff we come from—
        gather for astral copulation;
          snippets of stellar
sperm are sucked inside black holes
so powerful all matter vanishes and may end up
down or sideways in someone else's universe.
Finally, electrons reach us from these
        birthed beacons after
        billions of years,
galactic firecrackers popping off,
        flashing their signatures
like flaming Vikings set afloat on boats
pitching on an undulating sea
that may indeed curve time
        back to its beginning.

THE LATEST ILLUSION

A MINIATURE LIFE

At 3 A.M., when voices become internalized,
we sometimes get an idea who we really are.

At the end of a night of inapposite dreams,
irrational fears recant like darkness
after it is summarily removed by an aroused sun.
Morning conveys purpose, the latest illusion
retreats into subconsciousness.
It is time to shave or apply makeup,
down a quick breakfast, travel to plant,
school, or onto the fields.

Change and choice are linked,
understood when a certain heat emanates from the moon,
especially when it rises
shortly after sunset, its face rounded,
sort of grinning,
something you can understand better
after gorging yourself with sex.

Each day becomes a miniature life.

ELECTRONS AND BEAVER PONDS

It seems bizarre that electrons can travel
        backward in time.
The physicist Richard Feynman concluded that watching
his lawn sprinkler. Electrons are an enigma:
their mass is measured by inertia but not by gravity.

But solutions do exist. I look for some today
as I fly toe-stepping along the Green Mountains in my
        Piper Super Cub.
I trace the Long Trail, that brown-black serpentine
footpath grafted to the ridge in the message
        of fresh October snow.
        My favorite lean-to stands
among thick cedars and hides the small stream
that has taught my morning face to listen better
        to the woods.

South of Lincoln I catch sight of a series of beaver
ponds, each professionally engineered with a dam and tidy
        beaver house in the middle.
On a sun-brushed stream I spot a moose standing knee-deep,
looking farcical, chomping away at succulent lilies
and not at all interested in the fading red, yellow
        and brown leaves.

Eggs know how and when to become animals, some
animals convert grasses and greens into protein.
How does time curve, gravity work, and what about
      the twelve dimensions
      in the universe?
Night can conceal knowledge and dawn extricates it,
      but tell me exactly what light is.

My plane is balanced by power and gravity to remain
      in the air above the earth.
      In space there is no up or down.
In fifty years third graders will explain this
      in elementary terms.

The afternoon fades and is flushed with certain shades
      of colors difficult to duplicate
      or fingerprint.
I need to see as far as I can but speculate about
      a simple, indifferent life.

Rainbow trout flash and stretch for sunlight,
summer clouds bulge and swell, and rain spills out
      from a pregnant sky
      fat with time and purpose.

VIETNAM

Want to talk to me? Sure, baby.
You don't have to set your ass at the bar,
we can grab that table. Yeah, I'm real interested
in you, wouldn't have to come into this dive.
Soldiers like me hunt down all kinds of bodies,
except I'm sick of sizzling yellow flesh,
so help me, Mary and Joseph.
The kicking and screaming didn't
bother me at the beginning.
Christ, I need to stash the mortars and napalm.

Funny, when I came to this godforsaken place,
I was sure what I was doing in 'Nam.
Now trophies don't mean shit.
Yeah, baby, let's dance. The idea alone's enough
to get me hard, thinking about your soft, sweet,
beautiful stuff under the *ao dai*
or whatever it is you're wearing.

Your perfume's real nice; it makes me want you
like crazy. Your English? Terrific.
You understand me, kid, sure you do.
Here, let's have another.
My mother? Uh-huh, I got one. She doesn't even
know my sister's shacking up with some college
dude doing his soldiering on some parade ground.

My first time? You got to be kidding.
C'mon, Susi-san, let's head over to your place.
We can make like it was our first time.
I'll pretend it's a Murphy bed
and I'm the guy in the movies who saved it up
for the only woman he ever really loved.
Want more laughs? Like when I iced
my first, your brother coming out
of a hootch with a bucket of that rice.
Smelled like burnt cooking and sewage,
like splattered chickens. All over
that fucking trail. A real mess, guts and all.
Maybe I've wasted too many
of your brothers and sisters. Young kids.
Your guys have blown away too many of mine.

Sure, baby, no kidding, drink anything you want.
Yeah, and tell me your real name.
I want that bitch back home to know all about you.
What's that? Oh, you can count on me, baby.
Women say I'm real good. After,
I'll tell you how you can make it to the States.
Like that? Let's go, baby, while I'm not too
smashed. Tomorrow's going to be really shitty.

BYRD, RICHARD EVELYN, REAR ADMIRAL, U.S.N. —IMAGINED, FROM HIS DIARY

Alone, 92nd day,
July 1933
winter, 24-hour night
Advance Base, Antarctica

"I want my death to begin hot,
like early morning warmth that once
reflected off the waters of San Diego Bay
when I first learned to taxi seaplanes.
Dammit! I am owed at least that. Listen to me:
I will trade it without hesitation for all
eternity, whatever you request of me.
I am a naval aviator, an Annapolis man,
a Virginian, an explorer. We do not
like to express our feelings, but I am
finished, dead already, here in this
white hell where the cold sets fire
to your skin, then races to every joint,
every muscle before strangling thought,
freezing it into this diary I will
carefully place next to this, my last bed.

"I will die soon surrounded only by my
old companions, arrogance and ambition,
who cleverly kept from me the insidious

yet recognizable warnings. I should have felt
the Antarctic terrors that make the Arctic
seem like a weekend jaunt into the Smokies.
Every solitary thing consists of darkness,
all light gone from domed sky, from thinned mind,
pulling with it whatever is left of faith.
The voices of Scott and Shackleton clank
through the howl like the ghost of Hamlet's father,
their wails the suffering and frustration
of missions staked into the conspiring ice.

"I cannot even zip open my sleeping bag,
weakness overwhelming like the pain
that searched everywhere before settling
in my eyes that once looked down on soft,
plowed fields of the South where
children would hear my biplane, shout
and run to their mothers, who would watch me
circle as I rocked my wings through spirited air,
the joy of wafting an exquisite, sensual
gift I took for granted, but never should have.

"Sleep is not sleep, but floats in carbon
monoxide torpors, then nightmares demanding actions
from me; but I am defenseless, trapped and doomed
in this vise, timed to catch insolence.
I lust for light, any light, but possess
no energy to pump air into the pressure lamp.
The roof is caving in, the tunnel
smashed and barren, lost fantasies of survival.

Could I have been the man who convinced
Edsel Ford, John D. Rockefeller and Vincent Astor
to give me all that money to mount exotic
expeditions that would make me far more celebrated
than Amundsen and, especially, Ellsworth and Wilkins?
Ha! Could *they* take three months of
minus seventy degrees? No! Especially alone.
What? . . . Yes. Do you remember
when I lost that bid in 1919 to cross the Atlantic
in the NCs? And how I struggled to graduate from
    Annapolis?
The yearbook said, 'Go where he may, he cannot
hope to find the truth, the beauty pictured in his mind.'
What I wrote about has finally come down on me:
the Arctic, lonely as a tomb, remote and detached
as a star. I have never experienced fear like this.

"Please let me go topside one last time,
observe the uncanny dark radiance of whiteness,
take readings (you know I must take readings!),
face the indifferent wind, plead with my wife
and children to forgive me, forgive my selfishness.
My colleagues at Little America, Poulter
and Murphy, are wondering what kind of leadership
caused Byrd, that meticulous organizer, to require
this trial. Trying to prove he can do it alone?

"I will not tell them anything, how impossible,
how much trouble I am in—but, yes, they do know.
If those men decide they must make an attempt

to rescue me, I will order them to stay put.
But if they manage through the night, I will report
it only got bad when I elected not to freeze.
Either way, I will be remembered as a loser.
In any event, you must promise to divulge nothing."

GEORGE "ACE" ALLIGATOR (MISSISSIPPIENSIS), NOW RESIDING IN FLORIDA

Hello there, name's George but call me "Ace."
Here, you can get closer, I won't hurt you.
And don't get upset when I hiss and roar.
Good Lord, there's so much you don't understand.

Look at me. Does my nakedness upset you? Ah,
but I like it this way, all twelve magnificent
feet of me, a sleek, effective lizard, the design
perfected over four hundred million years,
an illustrious, superb hunting machine,
a happy collector of fish, birds, and whatever else
I claim for my eclectic eating habits.

As you study me—no, don't draw back, come closer—
lounging and sunning myself on this hardened
mud bank before I must go, slithering off
into the darkened, plenteous St. John's River,
haven't you decided how uncommonly handsome I am?

I've figured out what you have yet to acknowledge:
that *history* may be strictly a matter of interpretation,
ambition and *ego* are badly mismanaged,
courage and *greed* are exaggerated and falsely perceived,
exquisite *sex* creates colors you will not otherwise see,
religion too often distorts the truth,
death and *life* are symbiotic parts of the same totality.

But enough pontification. Surely you must have some questions. Please, do come a little closer. The name's George, but you can call me "Ace."

THIS IS WHAT YOU GET

when you're born, an invitation to your own party,
a miniature life offered every single day,
an earth that's trying to do it right,
people you want who don't want you,
people who want you you're not interested in,
maps that tell you things you don't listen to,
personal garbage that's not carted away,
lights and flush toilets you take for granted,
old friends who are not and acquaintances who are,
too many red lights and not enough green ones,
things you find hilarious no one else even smiles about,
relatives created by some fiend,
and three hundred thousand pizzas.

ON BEING STOIC

> Based on the *Epic of Gilgamesh*:
> *In the year 300 B.C., Zeno of Citium*
> *surrounded himself with men and proposed*
> *that the wise should be free from passion,*
> *unmoved by joy or grief.*

Gilgamesh the King and Enkidu
the Wild Man walked to the River Euphrates
and washed themselves in the still waters,
a ritual of brotherhood. The devotion
between them was as impenetrable as granite,
their language singular and hardly understood.
They touched and everything became good,
their two beings merged almost into a single sphere.

Gilgamesh denied the goddess Ishtar, who was
given the Bull of Heaven to revenge herself.
She knew the King and the Wild Man
would kill the Bull, thereby enraging the gods.
They caused Enkidu to fall mortally wounded,
Gilgamesh to grieve and lose his powers.

The two men remained side by side for twelve days,
spoke of splitting mountains and battling their way
to secret waters. Then Enkidu died. For Gilgamesh
the earth was torn apart. He tumbled through nights

with no end, vulnerable like a man who has lost
his mind. But after, he fought the will
of the gods and began his quest for eternal life.

When we feel abandoned we must act alone,
reenter the forest, inhale once more
its sweetness and kill every demon who hates
the light. Being stoic is the courage
to stop suffering, ban all confusion
and bathe in cool waters, embracing once again
what we truly know we need and love.

AMELIA EARHART

"All right, this one last interview before
I sprint off in my sleek Lockheed Electra,
great distance runner, extra tanks to range four
thousand miles, pulled by those two handsome
engines, my Pratt & Whitney stallions.
Fred Noonan and I, A.E., will fly around
the world's waist, a trip longer than others
have attempted, across part of the South Pacific,
from Lae to Howland Island, a speck of sand
so small it's possible we could miss it.
After long hours lingering in a stained and mellowed sunset,
hallucinating, Howland will be a waiting lover, arms open.
My motors could quit like foolish hope, the suck
of the black wastes below the final reality.

"Please, no endless questions as to purpose,
idiotic 'hand-on-prop' poses, waving
to your newspaper readers who either
will not understand or else demand yet another
record, another feat of holding my breath.
I have a funny feeling about this flight,
after ground-looping in Honolulu, having to abort
the beginning. Harry Manning decided to return
to duty; was it that he no longer believed in the odds?
Fliers confront dragons whose lairs they invade,
Hydras they secretly fear would one day annihilate them.

"But can you possibly comprehend the rewards,
the spectrummed sunsets after the terror
and amorphous nothingness of fog, that creeping
killer? Or radiant Venus slipping off the sky,
setting slowly into the sea on a crystal night?
In early morning my plane has bitten into air,
heavy and sweet with dew, before being lost
to a sun that spreads new joy everywhere.
And I have looked down on a city still asleep,
full moon planted on the sky, dawn pallid as smoke
that drifts like time unwinding. I have seen
the sea become one with the ocean of air above.

"Let me tell you about other moons when they
peek out from rain squalls, when I play tag
with sun and moon, when the sky is rose yellow
and offers bridges of soft, puffed-up cumuli
filled to brimming, like love? Yes, alive with
the exhilaration of its simple yet short life.
Entranced, I loaf in the peace of sunsets
there to be seen; but in 1932, alone, crossing
the Atlantic, my altimeter failed, my height
uncertain above the dark recesses below. Everything
I ever was, was ready to be torn apart, splashing
momentarily, soon forgotten by fickle followers.
For pilots, freedom is measured in height and time,
to solve the numbers for distance, fuel and weather.

"You say I haven't chosen a conventional life—family,
children, and that I'm not simply a homemaker.
Are you also accusing me of being a thrill seeker?

"Overhead, I am free of the ground, apart from men
who state, 'You're a woman, you can't handle the dangers,
you don't understand engines, you can't cope
with mechanical requirements. And as for your
    navigation . . . ?'
I say to all of you that women are as good as men;
we do not need male strength or braggadocio.
Men have prevented women from entering medicine and law;
we had to fight our way into astronomy and aviation.
Now we must break records to keep convincing you.
Our nerves are steady, we are certainly
as alert, and women have endurance that men do not.
You try to keep us out because you feel threatened;
that, Mister, is the real reason. One day, male
pilots will admit flying long distances is not
glamorous, not when pilots must force themselves
awake, try to ignore endless miles, an inconsequential grave
always waiting underneath, hoping their tested engines
do not skip the heartbeats they need to hear and feel
as much as they need to breathe. Equipment does
not discriminate, nor allow women the slightest advantage.

"You stare at me as if I were the first, or the best.
In 1886, a spunky Mary Myers ascended in a balloon
over twenty thousand feet without oxygen!

And in 1911, Harriet Quimby, mysterious and green-eyed
in her plum-colored flying suit, rakish goggles
and monk-like hood, borrowed Louis Blériot's
50-horsepower monoplane, leapt up
to cross the English Channel, fog cloaking
the water like fright from a recurring nightmare.

"And what about my marriage to George Putnam?
Are you suggesting I have a sort of 'arrangement'?
Why does everyone have difficulty with the truth?
Look, what is personal between us you will not know.
But marriage for me cannot be a cage, a stuffy den
designed for bears. I would rather live in a tree.
Women see marriage as a cyclone cellar into
which they retreat from all their failures.
I wrote my husband on the day we were married
that we cannot interfere with each other's
work or even play, that I would not hold him
to any medieval code of faithfulness nor shall
I be similarly bound. I insist that I be free
to feel loneliness and fear or the mountain
heights where joy can hear the sound of wings.
My responsibility is to flying, my work, to
prove it is not dangerous, that it does not have to be.

"Men's games, like war, remain their brilliant
arena of activity, their last stronghold they
would vacate if they had to share it with women.
I once spoke to the D.A.R., after warning them
not to invite me because I would only speak my mind.

I said women help make wars, applaud the marching feet
of their men, cheer their killing machines.
I said they should be drafted, the same as men.

"Walter Lippmann wrote: 'A pilot's energy is free,
maybe a little wild, but all the heroes, the saints
and the seers, the explorers and the creators
partake of it.' I have followed my path as I resolved
when I first flew; yes, this flight will be my last.
I will make room for others, younger and not so worn out.
I hope they, too, will see the other sides of mountains,
ask angels what scissors they use to cut snowflakes
from soft white clouds. I have released myself
from little things, danced fast fox-trots and gay
waltzes, beheld resistless days and counted them fair.
I recall how friendly stars lent me warm nights,
Brought peace to my spirit and lighted a lamp in my soul."

TRACKS OF THE FATHER, TRACKS OF THE SON

For Michael Gordon

I

Remember, Michael, when I used to lash you
Into my rucksack, bundled and snugged-up
In your bloated blue snowsuit, flopped-on
Red hat, and furry white earmuffs?
You trusted I wouldn't let you fall
Into the cold, uncommon arms of snow.
I sang you our made-up song, "The Daddy and the Boy,"
About fearless and courageous knights who journeyed
Forth seeking every Arthurian adventure,
Defeat a concept we would never tolerate.
We'd wave farewell to tearful and adoring women,
Bend under split-rail fences, pause as chipmunks
Squeaked and scooted, as jays complained,
You, my Little Bodge, plump, nonverbal
Two-year-old offspring, who helped me feel
The trusted leader as I committed us to
Tracks I hoped you'd one day follow.

II

Today as I fly us high over limp, loppy clouds
Hanging over Connecticut, you sit thin

And quiet behind me, your thoughts your own.
We pass over sweet green rows of corn
And pragmatic Guernseys unaware of mortality.
You trust again where my hands and feet will
Take us as we duck and weave like boxers under
A new, thick menacing roof of Massachusetts grays.
Berkshire peaks struggle to break through
The lowering canopy to breathe once more in the sunlight.
We have to fly so low over the lush jungles of Vermont
I shout back that we might have to turn around
Or set down and wait for the roguish weather
To tire and move on. I glance back, expect
Concern, but you shrug and say with a puckish smile,
"You're the pilot, Dad, whatever you say."

III

We've circled the earth, haven't we, Mike,
Flown courses flowing with a bloodline
That rhymes and binds us through minds and bodies.
You see those two eastern pines down there?
I stand taller but you've begun to stretch
Past me with every quarter of the watching moon,
Soon to rise higher and travel much farther.
Someday I will sit quietly behind you
And smile as you inevitably carry me toward the night.

THIS WAY TO MORNING

This is the way to morning
but you must first demand light.
And not because it's an old habit.
Making love should be more than just sharing.

Slip away from the dreams you've just made,
particularly the ones you can't figure out.
The subconscious cannot always be trusted.
And don't forget to test the air for smells.

Understand what it is you long for.
But you had better be very specific.
Complaining is simply another avoidance.
Watch your child, you can learn something.

If it's winter, carefully remove the ice
from repressed branches,
and make the buds wake up and dress in green.
Listen to cool jazz and especially to yourself.

It's easy to get lost on this road.
It often turns and the trees all look alike.
So do the faces of most people.
At least now you're awake and you have choices.
Now you have choices.

THE READING

It's really terrific to see you again.
I'm glad you remember that Phi Beta Kappa
reading, my poem "Tree" that made you cry
and "Genesis" you said turned you on.
Listeners are supposed to associate
with memories they feel deeply about.

I knew a poet who killed himself.
Poets paint pictures, not just pretty ones.
Too many things drive me crazy.

Tonight's reading will include poems
about how every one of us is an orphan,
the torture and agony of Middle Eastern prisoners,
the slow murder of bulls in Pamplona,
the stupid crash of a fellow pilot.

Look, later on—after signing books
and answering questions about how to get
published, the creative process,
style, form, methods and of course
my personal life—let's escape, find a nice
raucous bar, get pleasantly smashed,
and fuck our brains out in my hotel.

PILOT

The way she looked, so radiant behind the controls,
just like she did before her first prom.
I can see her gray headset, the slick plastic domes
clamped on her like old furry earmuffs,
the tiny "mike" against her mouth,
a miniature bucket swung off a folded crane.

The way she scanned instruments, navigating
on airways to preplanned waypoints,
speaking confidently to Air Traffic Control
as she aviated on designated or chosen pathways
that offered very few telltales.
I remember her first solo bike ride; she was
unafraid but knew she would probably spill.

The way she flew blind in malignant clouds,
chin raised, alert, a smile hinted,
assuring me with her eyes
we did not need to see
where the mountains were or how we would
get through the passes so we could live out
the remainder of our lives on the ground.

Until that time when unexpected ice
clung like claws to her wings
and threw her out of an ethered sky
into the thick-skinned Wrangell Mountains of Alaska.

That day I would have flown with her but she said
she would fly alone, as if somehow she knew.
Now when I hear a plane, I try not to look up.
Now when I hear a plane, I try not to look up.

THIS ONE ASPECT

We sometimes try but cannot
really talk about making love.
We remember some things:
very personal, sometimes funny,
even the uncommon sounds we utter.

I often recall dozing off
afterward, intertwined,
never more at peace,
as if nothing else
would ever matter.

Of all the complicated,
simple, bizarre aspects
of being alive, this one—
making love, being sated,
relearning the enchanted
ecstasy of intimacy—

this one, I want to remember
after I am dead.

CHANGE AS A CURVED EQUATION

CHANGE AS A CURVED EQUATION

      I

The universe
      perhaps
      curves back
      and around.
At twilight my antique WACO biplane
          and I lift off
          my grass airstrip
To rummage around the Champlain Valley
        to be reassured by
        Otter Creek the Green
        and Adirondack Mountains.
We pursue familiar lines and circles
        for answers
But sometimes it feels like
      we could be flying
      with existence in reverse.

      II

Think of a ball:
      it cannot comprehend
      or tolerate
      the concept of corners.

III

Stephen Hawking
        suggests that the elements
        dance effortlessly in a cosmos
        of gravity and space and time
While we attempt to deal
        with events in a world
        down here (or up there if you prefer)
        that change and keep changing.

IV

Reality and change
        are linked like lovers.
        If you pretend things won't ever change
        beware of explosions
A big bang
        in your face
        in your heart
        in every presumption
Except if you believe
        you possess a spirit
        that protects you forever.
But does this spirit
        teach you about the curves
        and corners
        that define your life?

      V

Perhaps
      memories dreams and fantasies
      curve back to some beginning
      we might better understand.
It comes down
          to decoding
          the meaning of change
          if it curves
          or travels a straight line.

THE WAY FORWARD, THE WAY BACK

The leaf hesitates then pitches forward
From the ash tree onto my deck and acts confused
Not sure of its way down.
The way it's supposed to go used up
Bleeding away its rusted roan the green
Of past youth forgotten those carefree
Radiant rash days when age didn't matter.
Someone called me I think I was shaving.
I can't even remember who it was.
Something about money something about
How I should send a check how important it was.
I wanted to send busted glass instead.
Colored glass from the beach polished with reality.
There are old and new things to learn.
Like in that epic poem about Gilgamesh and Enkidu.
Would they take on the gods today?
Were they lovers or just inseparable friends?
Shakespeare should have written a play
About their tragedy in ancient Uruk.
I'd like to smell them in battle but my nose is starved.
Max my dog could; he'd understand but wouldn't tell.
All right I'll leave now with my brand of dissension.
Maybe join up with that law-abiding leaf
No less confused and try to find my own way
Down to that incorruptible beach

Where driftwood chronicles disordered lives,
Where shells remember former housekeepers,
Where salt swims and tastes time before moving
Out into the universe on its mission to deliver the leaf.

UNTIL HE ASKED ME

He flew airplanes as if he had to
    embracing them as lovers
coupling, merging, rising up
    from constrained earth,
like a whale from the sea, bursting
    flushed with the skies he adored.

    He was the father I knew on the ground
but never really above it,
    until he asked me before he died
to cremate the hell out of him, toss his ashes out,
    pretend he was taking his last breath,
    the one he would carry into eternity.

FIRST LOVE

that day noisy in the phone
booth the trucks on the expressway
I called you I did every day
wanted to needed to feel
complete my stunted mind
crippled with immaturity
a bad excuse for my narcissism you knew that
you loved me anyway
what others had to confront
you did when they told you
it was leukemia
gift gift gift wonder
daffodils rich gold yellow the sun
those snappy expectant April mornings
when we can't conceive of anything
going wrong you took my hand once see
look at this one it unfolds like we do
remember I remember
every spring your expression flushed
you taught me sometimes we'd pull
off the road in the bushes
front seat back seat against the car
the rest of the world abandoned
sleep we shared afterward in bed so many beds
on the floor try to understand you said what's
happening it's all right no please I

begged you can't go how can I live I did
you didn't every spring I kneel next to one
particular daffodil I say your name today again
I don't know what to do about the daffodil

YAQUI UNIVERSE

When you waited alone through the night
      to dream of buffalo and deer
      sitting on the terra cotta bluff
      you watched the dark winds
dispatch the stars into their sleep.

      When you witnessed the dawn arrive
      smoky-gray then change to crimson
      powder-blue then change to azure,
You understood how the gods cause
      the light to spill down into the sky.

Then you became the universe.
Then you became the universe.

MAKAH COUNTRY

I live in Makah country, my brothers, the wind and sea.
The mussel shell carries our song
Across to the April seal migrating north,
Its fur, its meat dark and lean.

The seal waits upon my prayer
To the Creator of Daylight, the One,
Who will decide if we are worthy of the seal
So that he will give himself to us.

The tall forests of the Olympic above us
Hurl down wild plants, medicines and evergreens
Filled with huckleberry, salal berry,
But mostly the great cedar upon which we depend.

My sister Keena walks the summer beach.
The low tide permits periwinkle, limpets, barnacles
And sea urchin; she smiles, her basket filled,
Her harvest from the past, present and future.

When the fish call, my brothers and I
Take our hooks of steam-bent wood
And cherry bark to pull sweet rock cod,
Halibut, the coho, steelhead, and blueback.

We trust in Thunderhead, who beats
His wings into thunder, his eyes into lightning.
When we need his help and that of the One
He carries a whale in his talons to our beach.

MATHEMATICS FOR A RAINY MORNING

Thick rain penetrates the stuffed air
        and scrubs it clean.
Every drop has agreed to begin
        with two hydrogen, one oxygen atom
        in perfect combination,
Free-falling, thirty-two feet per second/second.
They crash onto the deck, vanishing
        like spent cells,
Their eloquent lives consumed then vanished.

Look: on the pond, drops bang the surface,
Their craters expanding into circles that flatten out
        as if what happened hadn't.
Others will repeat this behavior, ordained robots
Balancing equations of moisture and temperature,
Fulfilling their responsibility to the constancy
        of mathematics.

WALKING THROUGH THE NIGHT

JONES BEACH

Let's sit right here, us just us, on our bed
    of scrubbed sand.
We'll talk without speaking, gaze out on
    old man Atlantic,
Watch his energy build into rhythmic waves,
    their lives intense but short.
Commitment is in our fingers,
    each one of yours entwined in each one of mine.
Behind us the dunes stand cool and collected,
    their hair, made of shore grass, dances
To smooth jazz sown into the whispers of the wind.

Remember how we used to laugh at existence and non-
    existence because we didn't know what else to do?
Now I must sit here without you. Last week
    I released your ashes on the water's edge
To recycle your remains with the atoms
    of beginning and end.

See, the sand crabs continue to create
    their hieroglyphics,
Messages sandpipers and gulls have learned
    to interpret and track over millennia.
It's dusk, isn't it, and for all the days
    that will follow. I reach for your hand.
I want to touch you again, just one more time.
    One more time.

WALKING THROUGH THE NIGHT

For Robert Monroe Parker

But it's not as though I don't want
to remember that early evening in college when
Bob and I decided to walk fifteen miles
up into the Green Mountains. That
weightless night spring was untroubled,
clothed in laughter because we owned time,
giddiness an attempt to escape
our sheltered cocoons. The sky warmed up
with early light as we struck the high meadows
woods the stream where we had caught rainbow trout.

When we are born next time we'll understand more
about pain and loss when you finally give up all hope
and slide straight down into a lake, your last breath
bathed in tears. We'll walk far beyond the campus
get married have children and love as never before.

ELEGY FOR BOB JOHNSON

old friend no longer you
stagnant in death
locked forever in your years

even now your whispers
differ from your old voice
I can still hear you teaching me
about the clever behavior of plants
habits and habitats of deer fox bass kingfishers
and the clapper rails you studied for your doctorate

you never accepted laptops
they invaded your privacy
we couldn't get you to talk with them
remember the backpacks when we camped
you made your own I never met anyone
who wrapped the outdoors around himself better
home cold hot snow or rain
now your ashes are strewn
into an upstate New York wind
and over a Fire Island beach

I have things to tell you Bob
a mink crossed my runway
two broad-shouldered hawks
were feeding on a large rabbit
the adult teaching its young

did I tell you my new essay
the environment woods lakes
oceans streams especially air
we need to offset down-your-throat TV
how they blast us on radio media ads
fired on us as if we need them to survive

where the hell are you Bob?
only a couple of months I'm frightened
I want you to call we can walk
the lakes the moors in Montauk
hike camp the Adirondacks
wherever you'd like you said
you weren't giving up you finally ran
out of energy too many pulls downward
god you were magnificent

change is the only constant isn't it
the tide has run out you with it
a one-way trip to wherever
those night talks history nature ecology
politics women memories
I'll remember ours you goodbye Bob

DISCOVER THE AIR

All this time
      you had it wrong,
      believing you could only
float on water, that you could not
make a deal with gravity.

Discover the air.
    It is thick
    with meaning
and carries you on Aer's wings,
its power like some kind of divine
omnipotence. You can escape from the ground
      liberated to float on the wind.

What do pilots seek?
      Some mutter that slipping
      through the air is like
      the rhythms they feel
      making love.

Some look and observe very little,
    babbling about the music of Elysium.
Others ramble about Creation.

A few quietly insist
        that when Death
        opens its doors
they will enter on the air,
           grinning with anticipation.

BIPLANE PILOT

Inspired by Donald Hall

He doesn't have much time left.

He's alone now, the long years have
    buried his old buddies,
    buried the flights they made
in those V and Diamond formations, those
initial approaches over the runway,
the leader peeling off the downwind, the others
following the way geese do in trail.
Flights to another pilot's country airstrip,
alone or with a pal, navigating by "dead reckoning,"
the old way, before nav-aids and GPS.

He feels like he's enveloped in the sky's pageant
with the same awe he felt as a boy.
    But times the engine became rough or backfired,
    or weather a sinister monster in front,
    even worse behind.
He would have to shake off fear,
calm down to ensure the right decisions.

He gathers his old bones, pulls himself
up slowly on the lower wing, then settles
down into the cockpit, not as smooth as he did
fifty years earlier, a time he's distorted somewhat.

He fastens shoulder and seat belts, tattered
helmet and headset, smiles at past memories,
yells "clear!" even though no one is present.
He turns on the electric master switch,
the magnetos and presses the starter.
He sits expectantly, reviewing the things
he has to check: oil pressure, engine temp,
altimeter, rudder, elevator, and aileron controls.
He taxis through familiar grass, turns into the wind,
pushes the throttle forward, the plane lifting
him once again into the air. He scans the sky
for his friends, imagines for a moment
they're there, waiting for him—
    and they are.

NEW POEMS

I WILL LIE DOWN BY AN HONEST STREAM

For Kimberly Sparks

It's early, I've waited for the light
That lets me inhale this morning.
A voice descends from the mountains,
A religious summons posing questions.

I will lie down by an honest stream,
Place my hand in the flow of messages
That will wash away the tightness of tension,
The tear of turmoil; the messages will make me whole.

It's not easy to confront the truth.
Uncertainties lurk in the mazes of the mind,
Abstractions emboldened when they risk
Exposure in canons slipped from dreams.

Two squirrels chase each other around
In circles, oblivious to time's fatalism.
There is truth here—a momentary assessment
In the net worth of a life's balance sheet.

It's never good to be analytical,
To tempt understanding when it's wrapped
In so many cunning variables.

The wind comes to play footsie with the leaves.
Then it's off, deciding where to fool around next.

THE SEASONS, NORTHERN HEMISPHERE

Start with the thin days of winter
When ice makes its annual frigid statement,
When living trees, bushes, and plants slumber
In a ground topped with cool gentle snow.

Move on, clasp spring's sassy days
When renewal is offered in rich juices,
When buds open, flowers show off their seductiveness
That we've been passionately waiting for are here.

Next come the smug days of summer,
With all its whimsies and capriciousness,
When light runs rampant, children race around,
When time fills up its flushed cup to brimming.

Finally the halcyonic and spectrummed days of autumn
When we don't see time falling imperceptibly,
When we put away those other seasons for the year,
When we face up to who we are and who we are not.

FIRST THE CLOWNS

For Jennifer Ann

First the clowns, the politicians, the warriors, the oppressed,
Then the historians, the scientists, the artisans, the poets.
Bring them together alongside a pristine forest stream,
Where the sun professes no interest and hides behind the
    clouds.

Let them curse and shout and slam their fists
And maybe, just maybe, they'll decide to put
Aside their individual conceits, their self-righteousness,
Hold hands, begin to dance and sing an old

Slave song about reaching up, moving toward the light
Where fire and ice sit side by side in mutual acceptance,
Where the notes of their voices become clarions
For a tomorrow that has long waited for hatred to stop.

THERE IS MORE TO TELL

There is more to tell—what comes back—
what comes back to me
are the simple sounds of memory,
the ones from childhood days of summer,
when we played in our singing stream.
It laughed as it gurgled over small boulders,
hiding trout we somehow cornered and captured
with our hands so proud so triumphant,
until an older brother or cousin would make us
put them back because they were too small even for us.
But we growing up near forests and fields learned
to become hunters and gatherers knowing someday
we would become the men of our clan.

There is more to tell—what comes back—
what comes back to me
is the sweetness of an evening breeze surrounding
the hilltop when we swung each other
around and around until dizziness took charge,
dropping us on each other in a tangle
of legs and arms and hands and breaths,
until the light fell with thickening darkness,
until the first stars bid us hello,
until a mother yelled "It's bedtime!"
until we would fall into sleep
so innocent so wondrous.

IMMIGRANT

I never was.
        I never lived
The stories my parents told me,
Of screamed prejudice, hated ghettos.
        Of children's fingers
Spread to grasp onto the new land,
        the new country,
The new language, the new ways
        to look and behave
Like the native-born did.
        To work, to marry,
        to raise children
Like me who never was.

THE WEATHER

In an April on my eighteenth birthday,
my father took me fishing on his favorite pond.
"Watch the weather," he told me as we waited
for the pike and pickerel to decide if they were hungry,
"and look assiduously at the weather in your heart."

Now, I notice when the restless grays move
vigorously across the land, carried by a wind
that bumps into all things in its way. And as
I cannot change the weather, I could not
arrest the slow, painful, inexorable cancer he had.

My father is gone for some time. I am left
to measure the grays that spread across the sky
and the movement of feelings inside my heart.
"Remember," he had said, "nothing stays the same.
There'll be times of gray but the blue will surely follow."

WHY BECAUSE

I am not why but because.
It's more precise, a better dynamic.
You cannot know what you don't.
Don't listen to those that pretend they do.
Knowledge fills up a whole life.
It turns me on like sexual attraction,
The only things you have to do is eat and eliminate.

I'd like to be your new friend
Until one of us must look the other way,
Dies or moves away, the same thing.
Don't let that discourage you.
Better not make plans.
God will laugh
When you assume too much.

Those who believe they can predict something
Step into the endless quagmire of arrogance.
They never learn that history
Is always past, always present, always future.
It records changes we may or may not want
But had better understand.

PHLOX

The breeze, my dear, see how they sway
In a rhythmic dance they don't seem to tire of.
    But you can't touch the wind, she said.
    Fancies like this one are because you're so romantic.
All right, I replied, but here, these phlox are for you.
I picked them in the field earlier.
    Thank you, she said, but they won't last.
Neither will we, I replied, but we're here together.
It will add to the memories we'll share later.
    Yes, she said, smiling. Yes.

HOW CAREFULLY I STUDY HER SLEEP

She is not aware how carefully
    I study her sleep,
How I watch her breaths that puff
    rhythmically like a small bellows
    in the rhythm of perpetual motion,
How I step into her dreams she does
    not know why she wrote,
How I step into her fantasies
    especially the ones
    where we're so involved
Any and all speech is excluded.

THE BED

Our pillows wait to be positioned.
There,
    I told her, at the top, deftly.
    If you like, she answered, but
It's the blanket that counts,
When we're together underneath,
    arms and legs entwined,
Our smells merging as they have for years.
I promptly threw the pillows on the floor.
    We will not need them tonight,
    I said.

A CERTAIN TRUTH

The sun and moon play this incessant game,
       "I'm here, you're there,"
       pretending to be buddies.
       They watch each other amicably,
One waiting for the other to make some different move.

It's a silly game. Nothing will change,
But they never seem to get bored with the same
       old habit.

Yet, here's a message we've tucked
       into subconscious,
       a truth we can count on:
Their performance will continue after we're finalized,
       (but even then not forever).

Certainly there is more, more knowledge
       that teases us into searching
       bravely for even better answers.
They hide subtly in the folds of metaphysical laws.

Curiosity contains three uncompromising components:
       inquisitiveness, oddity, wonder.

They stimulated
       a Copernicus, a Newton, an Einstein,
       a Leonardo, a Shakespeare, a Pasteur.

An Icarus, a Shackleton, an Earhart,
    who traded safety for uncertain risk,
    driven to know if they could.

SUMMER MORNING

The fog imitates the mist and the mist the fog.
    They couple spontaneously in the fresh morning light.
My boys awake and begin
    to dress their minds for games
    they love to play; their shouts will fly
Through the air like slick-arrowed barn swallows
    chasing down unwitting insects.

The sun, that sly old man, rapidly becomes focused
    and gobbles up the fog and mist. I sit next to
My favorite blue spruce, its moving print inching forward
Like the soft shadow this poem advances.

SIGNS AND SIGNALS

I descend from a line that courses from one generation
To the next. My grandparents crossed the seas from Russia.
My parents planted me here, their voices,
Mother's, father's, then first love's, toll in my ears:
"Everything is nothing, nothing is everything."
What does that mean, what does it tell me?

I seek the wind, but it turns its barren back.
I reach out for them, for you, confront an emptiness
So vast it's difficult to find anything that is incontestable.
What if I was descended from a different line,
Say a perennial line of righteous, resolute oaks,
Those keepers of clocks, swaying in the winds of time.
I hardly understand them; they will not tell me their secrets.

I peer into a hushed puddle designed by rain.
A face stares back. It recognizes my inquiries
And offers no answers, only asks questions that surround me
Like those voices that urge me to decipher the codes.
I pull names of ideas, things, people down from the clouds,
Spin underneath to catch their multicolored meanings.
Their messages land on my skin, waiting to be decoded.
I close my eyes and listen diligently for significant
Signs and signals. Soon I yell out defiantly into the wind:
"What I am is that I am here. I am here
And will remain furiously alive."

COLLEGE REUNION

We return to Middlebury after five years
As we do every five since we wore
Those bright young faces
Tilted up into June's graduation sun.

At our first 5th, we practically
Ran up the hill to take our seats in Mead Chapel,
Waiting for the old-timers to walk
Or shamble in, look around and smile.

For the older classes, their numbers diminished,
Their gazes less radiant, less ardent,
"The Strength of the Hills" a little more distant,
Grayed as the aging snows in late Vermont winters.

We applauded them, not as tall as they
Once were, a little bent-over, their lines becoming small
    crevasses.
We stomped for the men and women celebrating
Their 25ths—oh, that seemed so far away.

Today at the procession's end, he's there,
The lone survivor of the Class of '32,
Striding jauntily down the center aisle, resplendent
In his sports jacket, waving, savoring it all.

For him we stand the longest and cheer
The loudest, wondering if we'll ever see him again.
We listen to the president welcome each class,
Extol the college we love as he refreshes our memories.

At Friday night cocktails, we gasp inwardly
When we observe our classmates,
Knowing we are staring at ourselves.
We sigh as we acknowledge who will never return.

We hug and kiss and talk, feeling the warmth
Cherished all these years; we vow continued contact
But accept it will be another five years and hope
Most of us will come back one more time.

FRIENDS

Friends check
Into your life
Like sweet summer nights.
You want them to last,
But they will move on
Like the changing seasons.
Some will fall like stalwart trees
No longer able to stand tall,
Their deaths locked into memory
Until that, too, fades like worn-out daylight.

WHAT I SEE

What I see—what I now see—
are long oceans of time
blued over by a sky that is always
everywhere for everyone.

What I do not see—
is you tending to your life alone
    as though it was fated
      for us to go on apart.

SECURITY

Sometimes curiosity about
        unanswered questions
ends up like howls in the dark.
Imagine a hiker, lost and struggling
        toward liberation.
He finally reaches the security of a road,
        river, railroad, some landmark
        he clings firmly to
for a grounded place.

You place your hands around a book,
a baseball, a coffee cup, a lover,
any tangible form that reassures,
        limits that solidify reality
        and hopefully the truth.

BARE ESSENTIALS

It must have been a dream,
The pithy kind confused with obscure meanings.
Let's stick it under this microscope,
See if we can analyze its conceit.

What about time, can clocks move in both directions?
Perhaps it makes no difference.
Was the dream real—or is now the real?
You wrote that dream—remember why?

Let's take off our clothes, get down
To bare essentials. Dance wildly.

Here comes the wind, secretive, uncompromising.
Hold my hand, you'll face some truths:
Ecstasy, escape, errors, time, limitations.
Or pull your own out from your imagination
You've woven from experience and maybe instinct.

Look, the wind begins to eat your flesh.
Where are you going so suddenly?
You were born to leave, weren't you?
It's an old story, being alone.

SIBLINGS

Come, let's examine
    greens and blues.
They describe elementary parts of the world.

Green
    reinvents renewal and affirms life,
Spring the best example.

Blue
    is more complicated,
    spreading itself through oceans and lakes,
    inside ice and glaciers.
The fabric of blued sky is wrapped around the earth,
    with it the subtlety of
Time where ambition and expectation are often
        unfaithful.

Blue
    knows how to mix with the yellow of the sun
    and turn into green. Green knows the same thing.
These two are surely siblings bonded
    by color.

COME WITH ME

In my plane,
        into those clouds
Spiked with mystery.
Difficult to describe.

You're in motion, gravity seemingly suspended.
You could be upside down and not feel it.
Your eyes focus on emptiness everywhere.
Nothingness in a grayed void.

Voices arrive from flight controllers
        from another world
        and sound supernatural.
You keep going because they
        have commanded you
To pursue a predetermined but invisible route.
Thoughts of distrust creep
Into your mind but only for seconds.

        But what if
The devil, that sly bastard, has infiltrated
The controllers' minds and has conjured up
His style of fun and games,
Creating false readings?
You dismiss that delusion,
Remember your training.

You know the earth is really down there:
Mountains, meadows, roads, runways.

    Quietly, you fly
Your way through cold, dispassionate time.

FLIGHT TO MIDDLEBURY IN A BOEING BIPLANE

Rising up from that overly populated
Fish called Long Island, I journey
From South Shore to North,
From Bayport's antique aerodrome,
Slipping by Islip's Class C sovereignty—*Watch it!*
You're not allowed to get too close to me!
I lift to three thousand feet to cross the Sound,
High enough, I hope, to glide to shore
Just in case, in case . . . below, the whitecaps
Look like schoolboys in uniform,
Lined up in rows by their headmaster,
The northwest wind; at least there's no haze.

I reach Connecticut, drop to 500 feet to improve
Ground speed to break loose from the heavy north wind,
Now a more humbled opponent, its full strength
Waiting for those who must fly higher.
I wander over coastal cities no longer separated,
Assemblages, stylized towns and villages.
Thick and thin roads seem to track to and from them
Like veins and arteries to and from a beating heart.
Where would I land if the engine quit?
That high school track, that parkway, in those trees?

Farther, valleys and hills look like disorganized
Soldiers marching in different directions.

Look, there's the Housatonic River twisting
Through Kent and over on the left the Taconics,
Mt. Everett always trying to climb higher.

I enter Massachusetts, turnpike snaking below,
Travelers limited to lanes of concrete.
My steed gurgles like a baby
And reminds me just how free we are.

I seek the hills that hide Pittsfield
From the south; it finally swings into view.
I call Unicom, told they're using two-six.
I'm pleased they have two runways that permit
Landing without crosswinds, "ground-loops"
That wiped out quite a few would-be pilots in World War II.

I taxi toward the ramp, notice two four-striped
Corporate captains standing next to their Citation jet.
They gaze my way, a few grins, expressions
That say, "Hey, look at that; I'd sure like to go up in it."

I push my goggles back, a hand slowly
Pulling off my leather helmet (my father's
Is too old, worn out and fully retired) used to soften
The stray cadence of the radial engine, the harsh
Stridence of the wind and the wind's whistle through
The chromed wires that hold the wings together.
I lift myself lightly out of the cockpit,
Weathered leather flight jacket in full view,
A dancer's high step over the side

Onto the lower wing, then a graceful
Swing and jump down to the ground.
I've practiced not swaggering, but my body
Rarely listens to my mind's dictums.

It's necessary, of course, to wipe the oil
Thrown onto the cowling and wings from the 4.2 gallons
The Boeing carries to lubricate and cool her seven
Children, cylinders born exactly at the same time,
Symbiotically and permanently linked.
Then the takeoff, May's smells infusing
The carefree air reminding me of college springs,
Beer and blankets, canoeing, Middlebury
Coeds who wore their youth like fresh flowers.
The plane carries me past Bennington,
Manchester's Equinox mountaintop hotel a familiar landmark.
There's Chapin Airport, then Granville's.
I must swoop low at least to say hello.

Pico and Killington, twin peaks, are next, then Route 7,
The fields of Vermont, farms sporting wondrous verdancies,
All tucked between the Greens and Adirondacks.
I see Snake Mountain and Chipman Hill anchored
As they have been for me since I was eighteen,
Then Middlebury, solid and mature, its longevity,
The college over two hundred years old, committed
To change, and getting even better with age.

Just ahead in Weybridge, my tiny airstrip smiling up at me,
Remembering our games, its moss-green grass prepared
As if quivering with the rush of anticipation.
It's been a fall and winter since the bold wheels
Of the Boeing touched the soft sweetness of her body.

OLD MAN GREETS A SMALL BOY

He is settled in a brightly colored
Adirondack chair, wrapped in the flow
Of memories spread across puffy cumulus
Scattered on the bluest of summer skies.
Thoughts glide down from the Green Mountains
Dressed enchantingly in the manifold seasons
Of his life, finally making their way up here
From the picture-toy harbor peppered with boats.

A small boy appears from nowhere.
He seems vaguely familiar,
His young body filled with energy,
His face handsome, his hands
Thrust deeply in his pockets,
His eyes distressed as if he was lost
In a strange and menacing land.

The old man watches the boy carrying
A model airplane to make flights in,
To compelling places for fun, for missions,
Anything to escape the pain of his loneliness.

The old man calls but the boy is pressed
Tight against his emptiness and cannot hear
When he says, "There is nothing
Wrong with you. You have not failed.
You are not bad no matter what they told you.

You will understand when you become older.
Anger and guilt can turn inward on you,
Become a race—a life race—
When you lose your ability to see the course."

The boy seems to understand and finally trudges over, smiles,
Reaches out a hand which the old man takes in both of his.
Quickly they meld into one. I know both well.

JANUARY DAYBREAK ON LONG ISLAND SOUND

The wind is finally out of breath.

Crisped sky brings faraway objects
    closer.
Boulders sit staunchly, wearing cloaks of whitened ice,
assured of their places in the freeze-packed
    salted water.
A few gulls patrol the shore, rooting out
    helpless mussels.
Buffleheads and scaup are vacationing here
down from the north. They dive for fish then pop up
    like corks.

On the land behind the cliffs,
oaks and elms, ashes and pines are fast asleep.
The rhododendrons are exhausted,
    their leaves hanging limply.
Blue jays, cardinals, juncos and finches
crowd the overstuffed feeder, gulping down seeds.

Winter is at its deepest,
    time is taking a time-out.

Nature is playing it cool.

ATLANTIC SKY 33,000 FEET ON
DELTA #73, ISTANBUL TO JFK

We ride a magic carpet stretched across the compass,
Traveling west-northwest, crossing ten time zones.
Sunlight creates a seamless azured sky,
The kind that makes you fantasize you're floating in Heaven.
The horizon hovers below, hazed and indecisive,
Not sure where to mark its line to separate earth and sky.

Georgia O'Keeffe clouds lay lower, spread
Mathematically over a cobalt-colored ocean.
Like faces in a crowd, there are too many to count.
(None would dare be caught looking exactly like any other.)

At the bottom, the ocean is firmly ensconced, thick and flat
Except where large waves are pushed up by the wind.
They look like painted white-crested blue-tinted snowdrifts
These vanish quickly, pulled down inside
By an exacting sea that swallows them whole.

ACROSS THE GRAND CANYON AT 39,000 FEET

Time crunched this terrain
With earthshaking sounds
That would have blown us across the land.
The earth yawned 20,000 years ago and forgot
 to close its mouth.

The Colorado River, browned
With captured ancient soils,
Migrates and snakes like an anaconda.

DAY OF THE MACCABEES, MASADA, 164 B.C.E.

Dawn reaches in as expected.
Purpose stirs into action.
We rise to face fifteen thousand Romans
Who have come for our souls.
They will not have them.
We have voted freedom over slavery.
In an hour we will
Hurl ourselves off the mesa.

PORTOVENERE ("SINUM SPEDIA")

For Allison Lee

Ptolemy wrote of "Sinum Spedia" in A.D. 150.
This seaport washes with Ligurian waters
Marked today with anchored boats.
Palmaria Island stands fearless
Across the clear Mediterranean channel,
With its mystical grotto carved
From the Ice and two Stone ages.
Human bones and flint utensils
Once rested peacefully there.

This winter weekend offers sunshine and sun-dried
    quiescence.
Families amble on old paths along castle walls.
Men talk and gesture, some with cell phones.
He and she pursue the jetty hand in hand,
Oblivious to everyone else, stopping to kiss
Where staunch boulders secure the harbor and them.

COUNTRIES WE CHOOSE TO VISIT

Let's consider the country
             called Guilt,
That land where we need to embrace masochisms
So we can punish ourselves.
We try to believe that we can discard our
             dirty deeds
And pull a blanket of redemption over us.

We don't prefer restitution; deliverance
Never feels as good as the clanging judgment
    of Hamlet's father, Hamlet.
Somehow carrying the cross and self-
Flagellation is sweeter when covered with the blood
    of incrimination.
        You wonder why.

I once watched peasant women in Mexico
Climb hundreds of church steps on their knees.
They must feel guilty about
    their sins.
About being alive.

THE TIDE ON ST. SIMON'S

The hundred-year-old live oak has arms
So long they reach across the lawn
Like the tentacles of a giant octopus.
The marsh sweeps out to the horizon
Like a perfect prairie of Kansas wheat.
The persistent tide creeps up the estuary
The way my fingers feel along the satin of your thighs,
Anticipating that moment once again
As they near the place, that exquisite truth
Marvelously fresh and new each time.

The tide reaches in twice each day, never tiring
Of the trip, never whispering it has had enough.
I wish our lovemaking was always as natural
Which like time itself doesn't care
About moods or days or nights or what we've said
Or didn't say to make it right.
Said or didn't say to make it right.

NEVADA THROUGH A JET WINDOW

Nevada reveals itself
in brown green and white stories
    in truths enunciated
in wrinkled hills of burnt umber
in elevated evergreened forests
colonized by coyotes elk and bobcat.
    Whites saturate the salt flats
and remnant mountain snows select
what will remain winter-covered.

Roads are laid out in lines
that corrupt the pristine soils.
    They travel in directions
        leading
from one nowhere to another.
Whoever moves on them understands
that distance is measured in time
    not in miles.

We have not yet discovered properly
    how to interpret
the whispered songs of this land.
We might recite better the wisdom
    of its language
if we were Shoshone.

APACHE

Our whole tribe has gathered for this religious
Festival, the men returned from their hunt,
The women with mescal hacked from huge crowns.
In high-pitched voice, the shaman proclaims
The rainbow moving over us as dawn arrives.
It is time for our Mescalero maidens
To come of age. Clad in buckskin,
They touch cattail fronds and kneel on tipi carpets.
Their "godmothers" paint these young virgins
From cheek to cheek with selected pollen.

After four days, the shaman will bless them.
In his hand a special symbol: "The sun has come
Down to the earth, comes to them
With its power and gives them long life."
This is a good time to honor the maidens.

NAVAJO

Tse'gihi is the house of the dark bird,
Chief of pollen, who will come to us
Bringing his moccasins of dark cloud,
His leggings and shirt of dark cloud,
To soar over and hold dark thunder.

Our shaman will pray to the dark bird for his help,
That we do all things correctly so that
He who is sick will overpower the evil
That causes his illness. Then he will
Again walk in beauty on the land.

SONG OF THE SIOUX

A lone buffalo looks down
from the bluff.
He remembers when we spoke
the language of the wind.

ABENAKI

Your dreams seek
the sobriety of winter
where only the raven sings.
The wind is its voice.

CHEYENNE

The stars spread spirituality
over the land.
The wind points to the river,
its hands holding water.

COMEBACK

Our forefathers traveled roads
Made of earth and snow, trails that carried
Them to buffalo and antelope and fish
So plentiful it fed the tribe, the elders, women and children.
We knew of Indian raids; sometimes we made them.

The white man took all that away, throwing us
Off our ancestral lands to places no one wanted.
We fought for freedom; we lost, our people
Decimated, our culture in shambles.

Now we make a comeback; we have learned the laws
Of the white man; we fight on his field of battle.
We gather college and graduate degrees,
Win back most of what was always ours.

PILOT AFTER FLYING THROUGH A STORM

I want you to study this man carefully,
    Landed after a tumultuous battle.
His eyes reveal more than his words.
    They describe his fight with Mars
and his cohort of ill-tempered warriors.
    I want you to ask him how he learned
to catch bolts of lightning and spears of ice,
    turn them into victory then laughter.

FIXED RELATIONSHIPS

At my age I shouldn't protest so much,
But certain mysteries remain like old companions.
Why are the orbits of planets and atoms so similar?
How do cells know exactly what to do?
How did gravity decide to function?
And why and when did time begin?
Where does eternity end and what's beyond?
Enigmas used to peek around corners.
Now they grab me, pressing tightly with their bodies.

ALL THOUGHTS

For Meredith Felice

Radiance from a poem can lead
    you out of darkness,
Its words the same as those
    spoken wisely by the woods.

On a feathered path sliding beneath
    the evergreens
Or reflecting alongside a fluent brook
Or stirred by the majesty of the stars
    you will surely decide

That the time for haste is over.
    All thoughts become primary
And swim strongly on the breeze.